A Giant First-Start Reader

This easy reader contains only 41 different words,
repeated often to help the young reader develop
word recognition and interest in reading.

Basic word list for *Birthday Buddies*

a	he	says
always	I	sometimes
and	is	special
are	it	that
best	make	the
birthday	makes	this
Buddy	Mama	to
but	my	tries
coming	no	try
easy	not	very
for	picture	want
Grandpa	present	what
Grandpa's	right	will
hard		you

Birthday Buddies

Written by Laura Damon

Illustrated by Laurel Aiello

Troll Associates

Library of Congress Cataloging in Publication Data

Damon, Laura.
    Birthday buddies.

    Summary: Because they are best buddies, Buddy the
bear is anxious to draw a special picture for
Grandpa for his birthday.
    [1. Grandfathers—Fiction. 2. Birthdays—Fiction.
3. Gifts—Fiction. 4. Bears—Fiction. 5. Drawing—
Fiction] I. Aiello, Laurel, ill. II. Title.
PZ7.D186Bi   1988   [E]   87-10866
ISBN 0-8167-1091-0 (lib. bdg.)
ISBN 0-8167-1092-9 (pbk.)

This is Buddy.

This is Grandpa.

"Buddy," says Grandpa.
"You are *my* best buddy."

"Grandpa," says Buddy.
"You are *my* best buddy."

A birthday is coming—
Grandpa's birthday!

"I want to make a special present,"
says Buddy. "The best birthday present
for Grandpa!"

What will Buddy make?

This? No!

That? No!

"I will make a picture," says Buddy.
"The very best picture!"

Buddy makes a picture.

He tries and tries.

He tries very hard.

But the picture is not right.

Buddy makes a picture.
He tries very hard.

But this picture is not right.

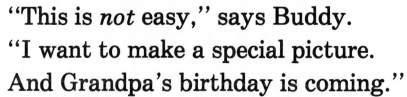

"This is *not* easy," says Buddy.
"I want to make a special picture.
And Grandpa's birthday is coming."

"Buddy," says Mama.

"You try very hard. But a special present is not always hard to make. Sometimes it is easy to make."

What picture will Buddy
make for Grandpa?

This? No!

Buddy makes a very special picture.

"Buddy," says Grandpa.
"You are *my* best buddy!"

What a special birthday
present for Grandpa!

JP   880026 04
Damon, Laura
Birthday Buddies